HEART OF DARKNESS

HEART OF DARKNESS

POEMS BY
FERIDA DURAKOVIC

TRANSLATED BY
AMELA SIMIC & ZORAN MUTIC

EDITED BY
GREG SIMON

WHITE PINE PRESS • FREDONIA, NEW YORK

WHITE PINE PRESS
10 Village Square, Fredonia, New York 14063
P.O. Box 236, Buffalo, New York 14201

Publication of ths book was made possible, in part,
by grants from the National Endowment for the Arts,
the New York State Council on the Arts,
and the Witter-Bynner Foundation.

Cover Image: "Couting" by Aleksandar Kordic, from a postcard design by Trio, Sarajevo

Book design: Elaine LaMattina

Printed and bound in the United States of America

First Edition

Library of Congress Cataloging-in-Publication Data
Durakovic, Ferida, 1957–
[Poems. English. Selections]
Heart of darkness : poems / by Ferida Durakovic ; translated by
Amela Simic and Zoran Mutic ; edited by Greg Simon. — 1st ed.
p. cm.
Translated from Serbo-Croatian (roman).
1. Durakovic, Ferida, 1957–   —Translations into English.
I. Simic, Amela. II. Mutic, Zoran. III. Simon, Greg. ICV. Title.
PG1419.14.U62S713   1999   98-39977
891.8'2154—dc21   CIP

HEART OF DARKNESS

HEART OF DARKNESS

INTRODUCTION

I recognized her from an ABC *Nightline* special about Sarajevo. Ferida Durakovic was the striking young poet who introduced an American television audience to the daily horrors of living in a city under siege, and when I met her in October 1993, on the eve of the second winter of war, she gave me a wicked smile, calling herself "a famous American movie star." Off we went to a café, where she announced that the literal meaning of Ferida was *unique*, of Durakovic, *foolish* or *durable*. All three applied. She was a kind of holy fool who spoke outlandishly—i.e., happiness is the main task in this war—and soon she was pressing on me a small painting by an artist friend. On one side of a shard of glass from a broken window was a hollow face on a green stem; on the other, a black figure, with two blank eyes, curling around the base of the stem and looming behind the head, like a three-cornered hat. My friend is painting the city, said Ferida. I can't accept this, I said. There's much more where that came from, she laughed, and led me outside. A firefight stopped us in our tracks.

"What was that about?" I said when it was over.

"I don't know," she said. "I don't know anything anymore."

Homeless for more than a year, somehow she retained her *joie de vivre*. Serbian shells had struck the bookstore she was managing and burned it to the ground. Then her parents' flat was destroyed, and

11

her personal library went up in flames. Usually we are just happpy to be alive, she said as we walked through the streets, sidestepping the so-called "Sarajevo roses," the marks left by mortar shells. Never have I been so happy to write, to live, to meet people, to eat. I don't have anything complicated in my life, just life and death. I have to choose, and I choose to write. She paused at a crosswalk we would have to sprint across to avoid the sniper shooting down the street. This is a war against civilians, she said, glancing at the houses on the hill, and calmly told me that eighty-five percent of the casualties in the First World War were military, fifteen percent civilian: figures inverted in this war. She could not stop thinking about the poet Georg Trakl. After the battle of Grodek, in August 1914, Trakl, an ill-equipped pharmacist in the Austrian Army, was put in charge of ninety seriously wounded men, for whom he could do nothing. In the trees outside the barn housing the wounded were the convulsing bodies of hanged deserters. Inside, the poet, who saw one of the wounded shoot himself in the head, was also preparing to commit suicide, though not before writing for these men "the wild lament/ of their broken mouths" the inspiration for Ferida's newest poem:

Georg Trakl on the Battlefield Again, 1993

Our dear Lord dwells above the planes, in the highest Heaven.
His golden eyes settle on the dark, on blackened Sarajevo.
Blossoms and shells are falling outside my window.
Madness and me. We are alone, we are alone, alone.

What shines through her work, however, is clarity of vision. Born in the Bosnian village of Olovo in 1957, Ferida published her first book of poems before graduating from Sarajevo University, and her literary reputation was secure by the start of the Third Balkan War. Unlike many artists and writers, she resolved to stay in Sarajevo throughout the siege in order to bear witness to what became the central tragedy of the post-Cold War era. Only in the late winter of 1995 did she leave for a short residency at an artist's colony in Oregon.

Invited to stay for as long as she liked, Ferida went back to her besieged city, making the dangerous trip over the mountains at the height of the Bosnian spring offensive—the prelude to a summer of Serbian atrocities, which finally galvanized the international community to take action to end the war. Within two weeks of her return, telling her boyfriend it was now or never (the Serbian shelling was continuoius), Ferida was pregnant.

"Why did I do this?" she said to me seven months later, soon after the signing of the Dayton Peace Accords. "I guess you could say it was the Grand Yes."

Ferida Durakovic's poetry is another form of the Grand Yes, and it is our good fortune that a substantial body of her work now appears in English.

—Christopher Merrill

HEART OF DARKNESS

I.

TO THE ONE WHO COMES AND GOES

We're alone under the sky;
and we need one more secret?

You want to be like a dot
at the crossroads.
Even the fountains have stopped their tears,
and calmed down
between the sky and this poem.

From the high fence, from madness,
my years run away...
Madness: forgetting the dark depths
of the carriers of the day.

Our bodies are phosphorously alone.
Like frightened birds,
    our thoughts of encounters escape—
everything outlined by darkness.
Under the sky. Under the sky.

SOLITUDE

The clock's beating sounds through space.
There are no dead.
The vaulted glass has its door.

I count myself off.
I count from one
to one.
Behind and in front—emptiness
gapes, painfully deep.

 On my mother's breasts
waits irretrievable flame.
She's on the other bank.
Through the rising mist
I might perceive
        the warmth of her breasts.
My bank flows together
with the river.

The pulse's beating sounds through space.
A tireless lonely woman
draws tiny embroideries
        inside me.

Because of her, my silver poem
is imprisoned in ink.

METAMORPHOSES

I know: everything must happen
according to the established disorder.

The hero goes blind
after the victory.
Rainbows visit his body,
but he caresses gold buttons
and medals
with the remains of his hands.

Legs on the ground up to the knees,
hands in a state of siege,
and looking down on his ships,

the hero hurries
toward the dangerous,
besieged towns.

And accidentally
stops under the rose windows
and is no more
on the earth.

A FUTILE SACRIFICE

The eye falls
like a star
onto the black moonlight.

The night hasn't passed yet,
and it'll end
with the crucifixion.

Again: no one is attracted
anymore by distances
that have the color of fear,
and there are some flowers
that should be picked.
Hands are nailed and mute,
far from the rhythmical pace
across the living mountains.

Rumors spread.
"There are no more laurel wreaths."
They've been carried away by the birds
of some good, simple people.
There are no more laurel wreaths.

Here is another
futile sacrifice.

ROXANA'S SONG

It's evening, befitting for verses.
It all aspires to fall into me.
Autumn comes from the outside,
in soft slippers...
I'm not afraid, but don't open
the door gladly, either.

One should think of love.
I'll conceive a garden:
I'm sitting among roses
          in moonlight, embroidering
a garden and myself among
roses in the moonlight,
embroidering...

A shadow climbs the marble stairway:
it's from the story, one I've
been expecting to burst in.
The air smells of his step,
whispers: here comes Cyrano,
enfin, with a cracked skull
from which gold is leaking!
Silently he puts his hand
on my shoulder, and from his bowed head,
love pours onto the needlepoint..

And evening is good for verses.
It all aspires to plunge into me.
Autumn, coming from the outside
in soft slippers.

I'm not afraid, but don't open
the door gladly, either.

A BOY IS TALKING IN HIS SLEEP BY THE FIRE

Approach me quietly, world,
surprise me.
            When I'm walking,
let the clean recognize me by my nails,
by the usual cry, by a face
which carries smoke and dust...

Let me be my father's sleep,
his insomnia, his childhood,
and the other.
            For the soul's
gold coin, give me a bit of everything.
Tomorrow at the door, wait for me
with a smile and sterling silver.

I'll give you even the chalk
from my fingers. And sense.
And memory.
            I'm one who's afraid
when caught by dark and hunger
on the road, one of those,
in the inns, who'll always find
the same face in a different dream.

The wise orange is being divided
among those of us who deserve it.

I approach you quietly, world,
to *not* surprise *you*.

25

PAWNSHOP

A big spider crosses my face—
the trite meaning of objects
and houses. This is how one learns
to forget things and people.

Former infants play on the lawns;
an endless horse neighs on the hills,
turning fire into water, water
into chasm, chasm into nothing.

I can't save the fatigued body
of the rose: the rose of the dust.
The rose of the voice I listened to
in my dream, on the knees
of a carefully devised Cyrano.

That thought limps to the corner
where I've met a pock-marked student
of literature—the future
"minor poetess."
                        Shame overcomes me:
how will I save the mirror
in which my image blows up?
More and more often I get attacked

by sleep, wipe little flowers
from the wallpaper, eat more.
The small house and garden
fade away, confined by the universe.

I pace through my town and see:
there is too little hunger in embraces.
It's painful to feel like a caryatid.
In my raised hands
I already store antiques:
frail wedding glasses, smiling bodies,
officers' uniforms, larvae and imagoes.
Imagoes. Images.

1978

EPISTLE FOR MY FRIENDS

...while (for so long now) a murky thief
comes from the lake to loot,
you wonder: do I stand on the shore
and cover the terrible surface
with a scarf? Or blow the ships off
the palm so he can meet them
while still dreaming about you?

In a hot sleep my cold hand
prepares your good-bye.
We'll walk—a lot longer—
like drops down the windowpane;
with clear palms, with pet names...
I was a hairpin in your hand,
in the smell—
                incense with dissolved salt.

Again and again we stop
before crooked trees in the park,
listening: an unknown world breathes
beside us. Beneath my tired eyelids,
I hide that world, that vague place
in which I must continue to change,
but we'd better sleep...

It's evening, the end of autumn.
As if love is seeking refuge
in your quiet scream
while we go down the windowpane.

THE ART OF THE GAME

I remember the day when wizards
passed through our town.
What to say besides that?
To sound reasonable,
to sound like readings
of a daytime soul
when I pronounce good evening
and good night over books,
over books...

In the shopwindows I remember:
this is my face.
                Then I scroll down
into the history of soul:
I'm the sum of all your faces,
acrobats!
What drives me into the game
drives me into nausea after the game.
Each of you measures my face,
telling his fear.

It's the same to you, like when
I close books
and put them on the shelves,
looking for a familiar refuge.
What can I do with this empty harmony?
I turned, inverted it...

But it is easier to walk
across tightropes
than to cross a deaf room.

THE ART OF THE GAME (2)

(In front of the Natural History Museum)

To accept even closed doors as a gift!
Three nervous solitudes full of books
and fear: we divide ourselves
into three small towns.

First, a park guard. Today he's got,
what, an edict in his pocket.

He watches a man leaning against a wall,
plunging into the façade, escaping, not knowing;

a woman lengthening the road with her body,
who's waiting anyway, waiting, not knowing.

Among the butterflies nailed to the wall,
she could have fallen in love.

1980

GEORG TRAKL IN FRONT OF MY MIRROR

There are evenings when I lie
in bed, reconciled with a thought:
I won't wake up again.
A hand with ether falls over my face;
a futile jerk and then
inevitably brave
I sink
into sleep...

In the mornings, at the point
where day grows, I feel painful
movements; I hear the staff murmur,
the body awaken. I see
the table and the chair
are table and chair again,
father is father again,
books are still books!

A passing day lights
the suspicious transformation
of reality: everything
is merely similar to what I see!

There are evenings that pierce
the heart of the day:
by repetition
they become so unusual.

TO THE ANTELOPE

I've gathered the remains of my soul,
atom by atom, and what have I found?
Everything present resembles
a cracked bowl of salt.

I practice for the big leap,
my golden dream. Stars! Close to me
because I strive to get above them.

I'm not a scream, or a fire.
It all happens more quietly
if condensed in a metaphor:
How it is to get fat and think
of a boil ripening on the sole
in autumn.
                    Then they are equally
distant: coffee in a cup,
an antelope, the space above the stars—
each step must make sense because it hurts.

I separate friends from wounds
and save them for tomorrow.
In the meantime I doze in the cradle
which my mother always drags
from room to room, whispering:
Hush little baby, hush...

ELEGY

I've made everything of skin and nerves
recently, on the Childhood Day:
a home, a fire at home, and myself
in the midst of the fire.

With maturity I add music, color,
and people. What I have is minute,
and for conquering the world,
nothing new: a dream which lures
like sweet dizziness.

Only my soul throws millet
for the birds onto the sandy path
in the park, cunningly choosing
the right one among all the chirps.

There is time to sadly confuse
the meanings of our destinies, "we"
whose hearts are bloody flags
from distant masts, people who
don't travel...

From home to the first threshold,
it will be a difficult sailing,
oh, luggage, and people everywhere,
in joints, in blood, under the nails.

The world's impaired
because I keep it warm.
It nests at the nape of my neck
in a secret rose.
                    I jump up
from sleep to see
if it still hurts in the same place.

THE HUNTER

I thought: I know everything.
In the dream the distance
to your palm was the same
as to the other town.

I picture a dark area,
listening to others
            speak nicely of you.
You walk on the seashore
with the satiated dog and say:
I'm here to protect you.

And black knights ravage our palace,
sell golden goblets in the market.
They've drunk the wine—
the poison that multiplies them...

Through the rose garden, the wind
whispers: Are you afraid of
death? Are you afraid of life?
The white tree, above the head
in the dream , collapses in
reality. It's autumn
and the plant seeks protection.

You, however, with the satiated dog
on the seashore, repeat:
I'm here to protect you...

THE DOE

A girl with a silent pearl in her voice,
a small girl, already fearing loneliness,
who scatters tenderness over me like down
so I fall more softly in the fall...

In my hand the dark is small,
and I know why: blackness peels off
from her smooth skin. In her eyes
it thickens in a sad rose.

Winter will be coming soon,
blindfolded, hands stretched out.
I'll throw her into the world.

II.

JANUARY 24, 1987

So, summer dawned this morning.
Through the frost and a scream
Marina Tsvetaeva
drew a circle on the compartment window
with her finger
instead of me.

A RUSSIAN STORY

You sleep, dead with fatigue. I'll dream:
steppe and moonlight. Bloody trace
of an unloved soldier,
                    red scarf
on white snow. His breast
on which a picture blazes—
                    right here,
where the bullet whizzed through her smile,
finding its peace, and his,
in the heart's nest... Good night, Anton.
Tell me your new story tomorrow.
I'll be jumping around you, happy
to see my dream for the first time.

NOBEL PRIZE 1987

(Letter from a young poet, to Joseph Brodsky)

Here I am, to begin at the beginning.
With no memories, no face.
        I get along in age,
lean and ripe, for *Ripeness is all*.
After my *I'm off* there's no comma,
no exclamation mark.
            Well, all right, my dear...
Only going matters.

I'll go. Neither slender nor with a silver bow.
The same. Not even wishing that other fruits
ripen there. I don't even want the road
to be the clean one on which those better
and braver than I am will die.

It's like this for everyone: November, cold,
and fall. Only for some it's better, or worse
to build their hunger on someone else's satiety.
I've had enough. I'm off. I close the tearful
           windows

and sit across from the tiny fire. I mean,
I'm already going: there, steppe, and Joseph,
and the dear Petersburg smile.

And so every day
        I depart. *Semper idem.*

The rider from this poem leaves a trace
on the path by the house.

FEDERICO'S SONG

She waited on the hills of the poem,
warming her greasy fingers on the fire
of our words. The soldiers from the poem
set off. She waved—not a sickle but a flash
of the sickle in the dark—the lightning
that cuts our sky into night and night.
And she'll wait so that her waiting
might be paid for outside the poem.

Soldiers in the poem marched by me,
stamping their feet as if in a dance.
I was cold in my stomach, in my mouth,
in the soldiers who were saying:

To war! To battle! (To the poem!)
Cover yourself with your flag
in battle and in the grave!
We know the roads. They're all the same.

Death stayed behind us, which means
that it awaits us before we arrive,
each at his own Cordoba.

TO DARIO DZAMONJA, ON JANUARY 18, 1983

Dear Dario! Look down your street:
five fair maidens passing could be yours...

But down your street, five winged horses
swept those maidens toward the enchanting South...

There, in front of your door,
they spat out five tiny pearls,
 a pencil, and a beer.
                    Run, Dario!
Take pencil and beer to your room,
the rest are fables for different children.

No one but you will have so much:
an unrealized world! At least that much
I can promise you while your dear
hoarse laughter teaches us
the pale face of nothingness.

And for that, that you are alive,
pardon my words...

(Postscript)

            And in reality it happened like this:
On January 18, 1983, in Dario's, i.e., in
Ernest Hemingway Street, I met five co-eds
from the Faculty of Philosophy, all "from
the sticks," and each and every one of them

dressed and shoed up to kill. They were
swearing and laughing so loudly that I was
ashamed of knowing them. Then two cars came:
inside were three drunken, middle-aged men,
two in one car, and one in the other. They
looked as if they were getting wings when the
before-mentioned co-eds joined them. Just be-
fore leaving—and I think they went southward,
because the weather in Sarajevo was cold and
unpleasant—a beer bottle flew out of one of
the cars right in front of Dario's door, and
the string of artificial pearls belonging to
one of the co-eds snapped as she was entering
the car and spilled on the asphalt. The pencil,
which Dario has to run for and take to his room,
the call of nothingness, unrealized world, and
all sorts of funny things, are *licentia poetica*,
so the author energetically apologizes for mixing
up this freedom license and the facts.

A TINY MORNING WITH A DEDICATION TO S.

The tiny sky is slippery this morning.
Across it, dear shepherd Perun
drives tiny sheep.

                    You go for
a walk, barefoot, softly treading
the tiny path. Here and there
a tiny glass, a tiny paper,
a tiny stone, a tiny hole...
This town is tiny, its tiny
streets are narrow—
                    how cramped it is!
And everything hurts you!

Reduce yourself first,
to human measure,
to earthly standards.
Only then go out for a walk.
With your bare foot, tread firmly
down the street,
stepping on broken bottles,
old newspaper, sharp stones, holes...

This town will be big then,
and its streets wide,
and the field
will be wide for a spacious,
virile scream.
                    The skies will be

gloomy: closed. Perun, The Mighty
Thunderer, will drive mighty herds
across them.

         May nothing,
my dear, hurt you... But the thunder.

EPISTLE, THREE TIMES A DAY, HUNGER AFTER A MEAL

For Z.M.

I write you from the vicinity,
incapable, like everyone else,
of giving new form to youth
that's coming to an end.
                              I'm not well.
I coat the walls with my hands
and the moisture from my eyes.

I eat with the choosiness
of a sick old man, so that food
doesn't hurt my interior silkiness.
Only water...only water
glides down my throat with joy, cooing...

But about the body—*basta!*
It doesn't deserve even this much
because it's still young, because
to be young means to have every shape...

Through the windowpane I see
the house across becoming darkness
and the man in front of it
plunging into that darkness,
into Bachelard's *illusion of warmth...*

I would like to see his face,
and for that face to become a house

which becomes darkness, and for me
to plunge into that darkness,
into *illusion*... But this is already
the weakness of a loner...

And what about you? Do you
come out of your rooms when the day
crumbles? Can you be found in
the steep and narrow streets
of the town? Do you fall as
darkness falls, imperceptibly
and inevitably?
Does your body serve you,
and your head, young waitress?

Does my love awaken you
from sleep, like a sword flash
from which all gets lighter
for an instant (so the dark
can be denser, so the darkness
can be thicker)...

You see, even questions
get more general
as the years between us grow.
And the questions I've asked
are leisurely like a poet
looking for subject matter,
not answers!

Stay well

for me, as best as you can.
The day is close, but this
is not a metaphor.
With your tepid hand I'll remove
wrinkles, loneliness, and this
letter from my forehead.
                    A pitcher   .
smiles from the corner of the room...

September 1985

PAPER TEA

It's not something you die of—
waiting for evening to fall,
huddled around yourself
like family in a dining room.
Real people die of something else!
On the shores, in the fields,
in the jungle—
                    of water,
of thunder, of tiger.

And you—you'd end your life
by a tiger's skin flashing
in the darkness!
                    Nicely and quietly;
no bleeding, no screaming...
The way it's done in the books...
As on the wing of the Snow Queen...

But wait a while. Summer evening
will start to fall over town,
over things, over us.
We shall drown sorrowfully,
flooded with sleep.

You'll wake up, dust on your desk.
Yet the better ones will die
of something else: on the shores,
in the fields, in the jungle—
of water, of thunder, of tiger...

LORD

Finally I know that my lover,
my righteous and courageous husband,
exists. For it's not his fragrant step
that makes me happy, but the pure thought
of his step, the fragrant one.

My lover, I know for sure, exists.
For it's not his firm body that warms me,
but the happy thought of his firm body...
I know I also exist, finally,
for it's not my lover that makes me happy,
but the wonderful thought of myself
waiting for my darling
that makes me happy!

Lord, don't forget:
Perhaps I do you a favor
by turning to you so happily.

WITHOUT A WALK

For B. V.

I write to you from all directions,
so that you'll be protected from everything
but my words... And the words
should be chosen slowly, carefully,
like peaches in the market: one

big, like sun through morning mist;
the second, the freshest, eaten most
finely; the third, the small one, with a tiny
trembling leaf, frightened of the crowd
in the market, with a drop of dew
that hasn't managed to flee to the sky...

Then another one, green, the one
which threatens, after lying in a warm place,
to surpass the others in beauty
and freshness—if the one who'll eat it
is patient... And so on

peach after peach...
          When Hecate
taps on your pane, you may bring
the gifts out: small ripe suns
which will break her black heart.

That's why I write to you
from all directions:
so that you are protected
from everything but my words...
That's why they should be chosen...

December 1985

FROM THE TEXTBOOK OF SLAVIC MYTHOLOGY

When the conquerors, monotheist,
unimaginative, tore and burned
Perun, made of Slavic linden, to prove
that there was no God in a tree—

they, half-witted, never suspected
that only God could allow something
like that to himself and to them;
that only on the fire of a divine body
could they be warmed up and fed.

There's thunder in every tree,
and in all thunder—Perun,
who burns his own body;
      and in
every Perun, a Slav, who calls out
his earthly sorrows under the linden.

III.

LAKE PALIC

The water is calm. And Joseph's verses
about fish are sleeping with fish, the lake
mud is sleeping, small boats are sleeping...
And the moon is trembling on the water,
trembling from what is seen on the water...

I'm just a guest now, a polite guest.
Therefore I'll leave tomorrow.
                              Leave the lake,
its dream and mine, leave my fear of water.
Leave everything.

And the landscape I'll leave
is indifferent. It doesn't say go,
doesn't say come. Only the guest tries to
        inscribe his dark heart. The water is calm,
        and the verses about fish sleep with the fish
        that actors will eat for supper, with pleasure.

I won't be here tomorrow—what a miracle!
I'll turn into a trunk, a passenger trunk,
        station murmurs, a distant tiny light
            where my sister,
                biting her fingernails
                    to the quick,
                        awaits.

THE GUEST HAS GONE, GOOD EVENING

One, two, three nuts on the table—
hidden essences that one arrives at
only by destroying the world.
And a lonely bowl, that is,
        with no oranges or apples—
the bodies have eaten their
beautiful bodies, and thrown
        their habitus into
plastic garbage bags.

So, three nuts, and the bowl,
and the guest who's no longer
here, that pure absence which fills
the hollow on the chair
the way it fills the soul.

One should get up, open
the window, let in fresher dark.

So, three nuts, and the bowl,
and the guest who has gone,
and sluggishness, which doesn't
let anything change in this
general picture, that destroys
and amazes with its simplicity.

So, three nuts, and the bowl,
and the guest gone, and sluggishness,

a dark eye, through the windowpane,
into whose pupil
        this picture sinks.

THE DOOR OPENS AND MY BROTHER ENTERS

I remember (I guess) how, tremulous, we
entered the cold little rooms full of future
plants, of cultivation; mother had goldfish
in her pocket and threw them across the room.
We would scatter to the corners; the one
on whom the goldfish fell would be that closer
to everything rich and powerful,
but be never rich and powerful.
                          She'd
bring out gold, armfuls of gold, full eyelids,
and scatter it onto the others in
                    each corner of the room...
                    Only Feda
wouldn't run away. He stood in the middle
of the room, under the rain of fish,
of mother's blows, kisses,and tears.
                    He stood
lanky and too bitter even then,
glancing anxiously at us,
with impertinence.

I was afraid: of all that happened
to him, of fish and pain.
                    Today, also
here in the corner of my room,
huddled by myself, turned to the mute line
at which two walls meet, I stand and I'm
afraid: the door will open,
                    dear Feda

will enter, waving hammer and sickle
toward the precious stone in this poem...

THREE GRACES

Three women walk the dark and narrow street...
One of them carries a lamp, limps and weeps.
Following her light, the others come and go,
not talking about Michaelangelo,
so let's hear what they say on the wind:
"Ach, men... Miracles cramped in the corners
of the rooms... And why do lamps shine brighter
when they pass by? One should have measured life
with spoons and gold coins, that is, beforehand
and across, watching what the wiser ones do.
Poured passion instead of fear around oneself,
instead of the tepid tear..."

Yet the one in front plunges her face into time,
losing hardness while lulling the other two:
"Good night to you, little sisters... One silk thread
for you, the other silk thread for you,
all around you, all around you...
                              There is
neither joy nor death...
                              The night is good,
it travels through us and surpasses us
and waits behind ages blue with decay.
Our thighs will decay into underground
boats which carry oil to the desert.
Our widened hearts will decay into moist
little nests where snails multiply. Our eyes
will decay into tiny looking glasses
in which the maids will gaze...

The night is good
to you, sweet ladies, time will surely shine
when it passes...
The world is perfect, *dream:*
in the parks, pansies spread their circus tents,
trees breathe, people pass, and every evening
is quiet. The world is perfect with us.
And without us."

IT'S BORING. THE QUEEN GRIEVES...

Please: just let something even worse happen.
Let the wind move among the leaves of grass,
or let the leaves of grass move in the wind.
Just let water, or scum from the water, move.
Let us fear nothing, queen, let us rejoice
            over something, at the very least, drought...

Lord, just let it not be
drop by drop from the tap,
tic by tac from the clock,
day by day from our hardened hearts.

Harken: the grass is growing...
Listen: a bread crumb screams underfoot...
The pressed heart of a rose awakens a sob...
The quiet, unknown,and tiny beings swell
to life.
                    My queen, put your ear to the ground:
The voice of volcanic powers gives you a sign!
A wise one knows what to do with all that wealth.
But what do any of us really know?

Grass, crumb, rose, living earth:
teach us how to rise toward heaven
without tearing the body apart.

THE DREAMER

Good night, little girl. *Dream.*
You won't get deep, little girl.
The worst is waiting for those
who sink most deeply, who drown
in a dream and at the same time
recognize themselves, whose breath
rattles from mighty dreaming,
from the axe that rips beneath
every depth.
                    There they meet
people from reality.
They defend themselves by flashing
the edge of their palms, and run
away to multiply
endlessly between two mirrors.

Perhaps the Tzar pardons them,
if they remain imprisoned
in the sulphurous valley.

As for you, go slowly down
your stairway, step by step
under the eyelid, mirror
by mirror, mine; don't be afraid.
Nothing's there, really. You have
all the dungeon keys, therefore

you won't go far. The last dungeon
                    is cleaned by the lunatics

who sink most deeply into dream.
Who drown in it and recognize
themselves at the same time.
Whose breath rattles from mighty dreaming,
from the axe that rips beneath
every depth. Only there they'll meet...

(Postscript)

This poem should be read in circles,
as the verses go, slowly, and with a lot of
sensitivity for yourself, until you start
feeling dizzy before you suddenly awaken at
the edge of a roof. If you belong to those
who have all the dungeon keys, don't be afraid.
The rest of you: let them fall freely, as deeply
as they want. If water, fire, and air don't stop
them, surely the earth will.

MORNING GLORY, SARAJEVO

For M.H.

This town, catching up to us,
clasping us in its arms
and around our necks—
we watch it from above.
We are momentary Caesars,
breathing in its breath; human
bodies, divine blossoms...
In the murmuring stations:
the calm of the Japanese
cherry in the museum
garden, and those who were dear
and nested in our bosoms...

One of us waves a hand toward
the ruined tower in the air,
as if giving permission
for it to be built anew, and says:
This is still an incredible town.
Let us go down. The face
of history ought to be watched
with more modesty. Only thus
shall we be reflected in
ourselves: How big were we
amid poverty and splendor?
Neither poor nor splendid, but so—
that, God forbid, neither befalls us.
Each tore off for himself

what the haughtier
and greater had conquered with a simple
and sublime account: addition,
multiplication, division, subtraction...

Then let us go, too, masters
of the air tower, let us
go down to the town, quiet
and hurt by everything.

Let us glide down the street's palm
like drops, so our dreams don't come true.
They're all the same: addition,
multiplication, division, subtraction...

* * *

How important it is to rejoice.
In everything! To accept even
a closed door as a gift!
                    And you,
if you don't know how to rejoice,
rejoice in the skill of one who does!
My precious one,

                    nothing is good out there:
neither place, nor time, nor action.
But must one respect that old dramatic
unity? A walk is for something else.
To go through mists with closed eyes,
like in the war, toward the sun,

72

to the hill above the town,
to the tower.
                    If you are ever
happy in this town, call me:
the presence of a witness
is vital for history.

In this town, in a cracked earthen bowl
from which tenderness and stench pour out,
in this incredible town there are trees
which, oh, joy, I say, grow toward the sky
like nowhere else!

                    * * *

(The day before we journey toward winter)

On a cold day a broken glass under the window
sends signals: It's good, everything is good
while the sun shines on us, it's good for
                    everyone...
    In the souls of the living, gloom retreats,
madness steps to the right, toward the edge
of the old forest. There beasts dwell, and only
they can get wild whenever they want.

Ours is the modesty of tame objects,
the peace of a house in the afternoon,
myth and history: ours, because they are
far from us...
                    I feel like crying

because of the road I must take, and yet
I'm all right, the winter sun on the wall
of the room keeps me warm, the need to cry
and to write keeps me warm,
                              to write my trace
in the snow, to leave a red scarf and gloves
in the snow, at midnight, close to the sick rose
which prays through the snow:
                              I am here, sun,
here I am. And there is no help, do I
also have to travel for too long?

Unprepared, we travel toward winter...
Old men protect their lives, treading cautiously
across the ice. Boys run past them,
giving no thought to the fall.

                    * * *

Well, there's no hope of your return,
so go forward then, courageously,
like guerillas through the dark of years,
across the morning cobweb, against your will,
like your brother who's now, just look at him,
going down into the mine.

So what if it's cold? Even the roots
in the ground need courage to grow;
even petrified bugs, even I do.

By the way, has July ever existed?

When was that chirping bird rolling
in the dust in front of the house?
You know, I think with love about a drop
of July rain rolling down a dusty street
until it chokes in an inaudible cough...
Lord, let it be my kingdom for a while!
Isn't it wonderful to keep on wishing?

January chooses its favorites
wisely: girls and boys—fearless,
cold, and joyous...

* * *

They are beating a man behind the railing
on the stairway.
                    A child goes through the red light
like a lunatic through life. Trees in the park
tremble because they are deciduous—
all of them do not depend on me.
Not even love: it comes with the winter
because it seeks a warm lair.
It dreams of something else while passing
through cold offices, waiting for a trial,
a wedding, a residence certificate...
For him, who walks along the shore with a dog,
still young, since he thinks about death,
                    day and night...
He and the plants speak one language.
Cut while falling, a flower
draws the line of his fear.

And my love comes from this world,
entirely. Tame, it begs for attention
and cherishing. It can hardly bear him,
made up of dreams in the nights
of insomnia, of silky
substances which shape his difference.

That's why he'll droop suddenly.
I'll describe his line of fear.

My precious one, far away
are the hills where your Beauty lies
asleep.
                    Since when have you been
preparing for the trip?
Since the notebook's first curved line,
since the first ripple of water
when you bend over it...
The sister has gone. And it's
unpleasant to describe your fear
to friends in the evenings.

It's better to pour your soul
into pottery, into
lovely dishes with a purpose.
Drinking up the other soul,
along with water, it can
happen that the Beauty
will touch your lips with her own
soft lips.
                    The heavens sing

the glory of the potters.

* * *

(S., town without the Orient)

Step in rapture and think of me:
I am the town. I am your face.
We are nettles and blossom in
the eye of the Oriental
slave girl.
                    Step in despair. I'll
think of you. You, lonely, tiny,
you are my face.
                    We are a crust
and silver thread over the crust
of the Oriental slave girl's
body.

                    Step in love (not thinking
of me) with the slave girl arm in arm:
only together are we a
small history of meaning.
                              I—
your face. You—the face of the town
without the Orient...

* * *

(Flight's child)

Let's go up to the town heights,
quiet and, as I said, hurt
by everything. Old enough
to fear falling, young enough
to be lured by falling.

The day is pathetic,
close to our so-called heart.
I fear for the others,
for my restless mind.
With palms of dust and ice cream.
With the town. With the homeland.

A huge rock awaits. This is
to be done: to fly only
with stones and curses,
from above and into
the muddy lap of the river.

The elder tree above water
would tremble, the bird would fly
off with the soul, the bright July
day would feel sorry that,
once again, someone behaves
badly to the river.
That would be all.
Then nothing.

IV.

BEAUTY AND THE BEAST

Untruthful Beauty
Slammed the door
Finally
As the Homeland did,
Then vanished
Into history.

Nonetheless, Beauty,
Untruthful one,
And the Homeland
Have something in common—
Both leave behind
The boys
Who will die
For them.

War, 1991

A FRAGRANT AFTERNOON IN JULY
IN THE TOWN IN THE WORLD

July has settled on the town.
The angels feel warm in heaven
and their fragrant sweat is falling
on a pale young woman's face
as she passes beneath a linden.

A man hurried past her,
and giving no significance
to it, thought: she is so fragrant
and tearful.

A child brushed against her dress
and looked at her carefully
as angels carefully look
at human souls—
Pletty flaglant lady...

Then she stepped onto the train
platform and vanished from this poem,
with all of her fragrances.
The night sneaked into the park
and the flowers closed their
small shops of healthy darkness.

Summer, 1991

THE HEART IS A LONELY HUNTER

Can you hold out with no fervor or fame?
Leave me alone for a while, and look:
the soul travels over moonlit water...
We are both alive, our words falling
like petals, like petals our words fall,
our words fall on the table like petals:
MY MOTHER IS ILL, MY FATHER, TOO.

I'd move my health from the right side
toward them.
                    And I wouldn't.
From the left: girls scream

and boys go down the sliding board down
the sliding board sliding down the board:
at the bottom a puddle awaits them.
In it: pebble, water, crazed tears on
Sunday afternoon.
                    I watch a movie
with a happy ending.
                    Genuine
revulsion on Sunday afternoon,
watching a movie with a happy
ending, can you, my heart, hold out
with no fervor or fame?

                    I can, if
you pay me. But not with futile gold!,
says my heart, grinning from the mirror
through my open mouth.

LIE DOWN INTO YOUR AGE, VLADIMIR

To V. Albahari

Transparent boy, his head
a capuchin monk's—
                    in
cold shelters he leaves impudence
and loneliness, and over
the town he carries off
impudence and loneliness
made in Ireland,
                    selling them
to some and to some, by God,
giving them away, kinglike...

Oh, how conceited and lonely
Vladimir is when darkness
starts crawling over the edge
of the table!
                    Tiny ants
traverse there
with the crumbs of his daily bread.
He's the one who hoards wasteland
like gold! Soon he'll purchase
a bit of God's grace for it.

Vladimir, lie down into
your age. Many others do!
Today let my smile touch
your transparent temples.

(Postscript)

Vladimir Albahari, a Sarajevan, a poet,
a lunatic, a cursed Jew, dreamed so much about
leaving his hometown, so much that we all were
certain he would never leave. He left, at the
beginning of war. That means that the poet's
dream—Oh, what a sin—came true. He had to
leave: his skin was so transparent and his bones
were so light that with the first shells he
turned into a seagull and flew over the Chan-
nel. The poet's dream, therefore, and his
town, are at a loss. Vladimir, naturally, is
at a loss. There is no one there to write
about him. I dream, as he did, that this
poem will reach him some day. In 1994 he
sent me a message: "I left Sarajevo just be-
fore the war, you liar!" And I replied:
"OK, Vladimir. I lied. But the poem
reached you. That was what I had intended
with it." And it was.

LOOK, SOMEONE HAS MOVED FROM THE BEAUTIFUL NEIGHBORHOOD WHERE ROSES DIE

A rose screamed, dying in sleep,
and from that a July day
was born.
               The heart of a lonesome
little spider trembled in
the corner of a deaf room.

Carpets, and clumsy, dusty
things abandoned the house,
carrying within themselves
life, stuffy and long.
               And love,
stuffy and long, kept falling
out of old letters and books,
onto the blistering highway
until, in a cloud of stuffy
dust, at the touchingly
ugly exit from town,
the heavy truck vanished.

THE TIME IS RIPE, AND IT'S COLD

I'm leaving, dear. There's too much joy with you!
My heart, a poisonous plant, isn't used to it.
There was too much pain, my "farewells" and
                           others' too.
I'd better go now, while there's still a trace

of love hidden in us, while the tiny
looking glass trembles, where you look at yourself,
looking at me. Thus—and only thus—some
sparse joy will remain, which warns us, already

stumbling past us, weary and mature.
For there's no superb love, flower of my joy.
It's gone into romances, promising
a warm home to diapers, sickness, domestic
healing tea... To the ghost, father, and son.

Therefore, I'm going, dear, to the other
room at least! Not to look at your looking
glass, similar to my laborious,
exhausted, well-ripened old age, my doom,
unsuitable for fidelity,
eternal and glorious!

I defend you with love from a romance,
crying because, alas, I already
have to go, having spent you as gold coin,
which was the only thing I had.
I'm leaving, my darling.

I've had enough of you, as you of me.
It's enough. Enough. Enough.

WAR HAIKU

***

The shells are silent
In the remaining treetop
A small sparrow chirps

***

There are no chestnuts
Under the blind windowpanes
Lengthy is the night

***

The grasses spring up
Upon the heated asphalt
Blood and bread recline

***

Late May afternoon
In the middle of asphalt
Two bloody roses

***

All my dear friends
Next to the fallen ash tree
I am thinking of you

***

Museum garden
Recalls Japanese cherry
We were silent there

* * *

An insane lamentation
By the destroyed houses
Where a dog whines

* * *

Bullets are whizzing
In the crown of the ash tree
There are no sparrows

HAIKU FOR A FRIEND

Dragan H. lived here.
Now he lives with the gun
of E. Hemingway.

PRAISE TO THE TREE IN FRONT OF THE HOUSE

Even you will die
Like Lee Marvin died!

He produced fresh air
Just like you do.

A WAR LETTER

(About the letter from before the war)

The Universe sent darkness to our humble home,
which is gone now. The letter, and every single
                    book,
and dear things: they all burned like Rome.
But it is just an image! Have a look:

We aren't gone! And manuscripts never burn,
they say. It means that I'll read anew
that precious letter, whenever you turn,
whenever only those few syllables

change our agony into an endlessly dull
winter afternoon. In those hours everything's
so simple that I suffer (same old song),
I don't love anyone, and the fear devours

me that passion, which brings back the first day
of love, the re-creation, is finally gone
like the heart grown in a poplar tree! And may
only this flourishing pain stop! May everyone
                    alone

leave for good, to wherever they want: to
water, air, or fire. And us? What fireside
awaits us in the times to come? Here is our home,
where mother can never tire of planting
roses and fruit, and us, her poor ones, on her palm.

A WRITER PERCEIVES HIS HOMELAND
WHILE A LEARNED POSTMODERNIST
ENTERS HIS TOWN

Cruelly and for a long time everything
has been repeating and yet everything
happens for the first time: the face of
a young man whose life was flowing away
all night through your fingers, through the hole
in his back. The face of a soldier,
near the bus station, with his eyes wide open:
the mild May sky has settled down there—
you're imagining, I say—it's not
the calm and distant face of history.

And a pool of blood: in the middle, a bread loaf
soaked with blood as if with morning milk.
I repeat, you are imagining for the first time:

heavy Sarajevan clay which falls on a boy's
big feet in Reebok sneakers, leaning on
the too short *tabut* made of a cabinet door.
No, you should not be trusted.
You have arrived from the heart of darkness
which burst and gushed into the daylight.

You are an unreliable witness,
a biased one besides. So that is
why the Professor came, Parisien
from head to toe: *Mes enfants*, he started,
and his fingers kept repeating: *Mes*

enfants, mes enfants, mes enfants...

In the Academy of Sciences
wise grey heads could think only about
his screamingly white shirt. *Mes enfants,*
Europe is dying here. Then he arranged
everything into a movie, images,
great words like *histoire, Europe,
responsabilité,* and naturally,
les Bosniacs. So this is the way
to look into the face of history,

not like you: in crude irresponsible
fragments, in a sniper shot which stabs the skull,
in graves already covered with tireless grass...
In your palms, laid upon
Edvard Munch, who once
invented everything, in vain.

Sarajevo, 1993 To B.H. Levy

GEORG TRAKL ON THE BATTLEFIELD AGAIN IN 1993

Our dear Lord dwells above the planes, in the highest Heaven.
His golden eyes settle on the dark, on blackened Sarajevo.
Blossoms and shells are falling outside my window.
Madness and me. We are alone, we are alone, alone.

EVERY MOTHER IS A WUNDERKIND

When we were leaving our home at the entrance of the town in a hurry, for good, I carried a few dear books, a vanity case, and undergarments. She carried two bags of food. I ask, What did you bring, Mom? What everybody needs, she said. Later, through the shelling and sniper fire, she went to our garden and brought lettuce, onions, and carrots to her grandchildren. Are you afraid, I ask. No, child, she says. I just think of my children and God opens the path for me immediately. THERE.

* * *

When my brother was sent to the front line, by our little house, she got dressed and went there too. Where are you going, Mom, for God's sake, I ask desperately. I'm going to help him, to make it easier for him. My brother barely survived getting her out of the encirclement. For God's sake, Mom, he says, don't help me anymore. Now she sits all day long on the balcony, watching and listening: Is he alive? Perhaps he's lying on the bare ground? Does he have anything to eat?... Do you remember crazy mothers from books? That's her. Just a little different. THERE.

* * *

When I helped them move, after living for a while on the fifteenth floor, onto the ninth floor, at our friends' apartment, she says to me, as if guilty of something: You know, child, I must make my own order in this kitchen. But I remember where everything should be, so when we return home (!), if God allows it, I'll put everything back where it was. THERE.

* * *

The other day, coming back from my "ramble" around the town, I grope up those stairs as if, God forbid, I'm passing through some long grave, and count: first, second, fifth, seventh, ninth floor, and suddenly on the railing I feel a rope. She opens the door, I ask, What's this, Mom? She says, I tied it so that you know when you have reached our door. Early in the afternoon she lights the oil lamp and leaves it in the stairway, so that people see what they are bumping into. She leaves the apartment door open, so the neighbors grope more easily in the skyscraper dark. She leaves matches by my bed, on shelves, on tables. She wakes up at night and lights the oil lamp again in the corridor. She knows I fear the dark, so I should have light on hand. She doesn't sleep at all, but all night listens attentively across the whole town, on four sides, with her crazy, motherly, hearty ear. Are we breathing? Are we warm? Do we have bad dreams? Is something hurting us?.THERE.

* * *

All day long, nine floors up and nine floors down, she brings water. Before the war she couldn't climb even nine *stairs*. Now, it's as if nothing hurts her. She is only two sizes smaller. Now, she says, nothing ought to hurt me, there's war. Later I will be sick as I please... The other day an acquaintance asked me: How do you manage to stay so clean and white when there is no water or electricity? It's all her fault, I say. She "fetches water," washes all my white shirts, sterilizes my pants and sneakers, and dries them. Then she prays to God for just a little electricity, and quickly-quickly irons everything and hangs it in the wardrobe. You mustn't look like a refugee, she says, out of spite

97

to those up there who chased us out of our home. THERE.

* * *

When the shooting starts around the skyscraper, we quarrel. I don't want to go to the stairway or the cellar; I feel better when I read during the shelling. All right then, says she, I'm staying with you. And she sits by my side, and I know she's scared to death. She sits until I get so infuriated that I also go out to the stairway or the cellar. I have never seen anything more stubborn in my life. She'll move me to the safe place, or she won't exist. THERE.

* * *

Around the beginning of the war, I find her in front of the house, sitting on a bag of sand, and crying. What is it?, I ask. Nothing, she says. What do you mean, nothing?, I ask. Well, she says, I'm ashamed that I gave birth to you. Why, mother, we aren't so bad, I joke. It's not that, she replies seriously. I'm ashamed of bringing you forth into such a world. If I knew, she says, that I must die for the war to end, I swear to God I would lie down and die. Just for my children and grandchildren to live. THERE.

* * *

With God, I have that godless, calculating relationship. She doesn't. Of all the possible calculations, she prays to God only to gather us once again around her, safe and sound, in her little home at the entrance to the town (!), and to bring out that motherly cheese pie of hers, which we used to devour on Saturdays, leaving her to wash the dishes and collect broken and scattered things which the grandchildren could break and scatter only in her house. THERE.

***

She scolds me every day, that I don't know how to find my way in life, that I don't know how to take advantage of a situation, that I am naive... I don't know how to respond, so I just say: Well, you know, Mom, I'm a poet, that's why. You are Mummy's little shit, that's what you are, she says, and kisses me again, smackingly, as Moms do, up to the sky. THERE.

***

And constantly, persistently, unerringly, she dreams the same dream: as if she is back home, and the house is intact, her flowers around it. The tomcat sleeps in the old armchair on the porch; she comes out of the house, cheerful after having a bath. It's Saturday, and we are coming for lunch. Then in the evening we are having a barbecue, and she can't make everything ready. My God, anxiety clasps her, chokes her, and she wakes up—in a crazy August war day, sweating and terrified, in somebody else's house, on somebody else's bed. And there, over the skyscraper, shells roar, tearing her old heart apart, piece by piece.

***

May God give you long life, my old one. If you endure, I will too. This war, like some long and serious illness, will end through your effort alone. You'll apply that secret balm of yours to it, that blend of wisdom, healing herbs, and ancient folk tales in which, it should be said, the winner is always the one who neither harms nor wishes harm upon others.

TEN YEAR OLD GIRL PERCEIVES HER HOMELAND
WHILE WATCHING THE OCEAN

For A.

I

This morning I took a long walk through
               the forest
which was made by J.R.R. Tolkein
when he was in a real good mood.
Then I sat there
on the sunlit mountain slope
looking at the ocean
waiting for a huge whale to come up
from all that water.
But he did not show
and I ate an apple instead.

II

Those (I think) who know what
I am writing about
will not need to keep on
reading these lines.
And those who do not know
what I am writing about
will start another war, back there
far far away, in my tiny homeland
which was also made by J.R.R. Tolkien
when he was in a good mood, but

ALL OF A SUDDEN SOMEBODY KNOCKED
AT HIS STUDY DOOR AND
the happy ending (which he was really good at)
simply slipped off his mind.
After he died
at the age of two fifty
        and never finished the story...

III

Today I am waiting for him
to come up from all that water:
somebody has to give an end
to my tiny homeland story.
I do not know whether Mr. President
can do something to make him return—
he has, you know, those Striders
and all that stuff—

Anyway
I guess I will just sit here and
wait for a while.
I think I deserve it. I have been
a good girl, after all.
I am just a little bit afraid of the dark
coming from far away across the ocean.

Otis, Oregon February 26, 1995

A CHILD'S MIRROR

At the end of the corridor
A child's mirror
Reflects a brighter dark.

Sarajevo 1996

EDITOR'S AFTERWORD
AND
AUTHOR'S NOTES

EDITOR'S AFTERWORD

The third regime, the modern one, is that
of indifference...
                                        —Roberto Calasso

Americans have the luxury of being pacifist. Lucky you.
                                        —Ferida Durakovic

Ferida Durakovic's *Heart of Darkness*, from it's "borrowed" title on
down to single lines and images, is a book that echoes, in a distinctly
modern way, the murmurings of great poets who have inhabited the
troubled enclaves of our century. Conrad, Rilke, Trakl, and García
Lorca are here, with Tsvetaeva, Brodsky, and their incredible, plain-
spoken, and indomitable mentor, the woman who also wouldn't leave
her besieged country, Akhmatova. As anyone who has seen
Durakovic's recent work or interviews with her knows, those cowards
who ringed her beautiful city with heavy artillery lobbed a shell or
two into her family's home, and destroyed her library. What she has
left, she carries with her in the places that still matter: her heart, and
the heart of her poems. Durakovic, in her infinite poetic wisdom, lets

other poets speak of their troubles and triumphs through her work, and wastes only a single, acid-tinged line on the pathetic, doggerel-spouting artillerists of Pale, spoken by her quietly heroic mother. It is, perhaps, more than all of the killers, gathered together in the lonely circle of hell that surely awaits them, are worth.

Like winter, so lovingly personified in her poem "The Doe," Durakovic was thrown out into the cold when the shells started falling on Sarajevo. She carried "a few dear books, a vanity case and undergarments." (The books were *The Little Prince* and *The Lord of the Rings*.) Her mother, that prosaic soul, carried what everybody needs, she said. (Two bags of food.) With her goldfish, cheese pie, fruit trees, vegetables and plants, Durakovic's mother is the source of her poetic fecundity, the one who so resolutely emerges as her perennial muse.

Working with her muse, Durakovic invokes the icons and myths of her troubled city. If they are fairy tales, they are also tinged with the dark inherent in a people who have been caught between the two dominant religions of Europe. *Perun*, the Slavic God of Thunder, calls out his sorrows under the sacred linden tree, which Durakovic knows has been cut down and burned for warmth. We're alone under the sky," the book begins, like Rilke's angel, and Lorca's first notes in *Poeta un Nueva York*, "Cut down by the sky..." For the besieged poet, the thunder of the guns narrows her life dramatically, but simultaneously widens her field of reference: "...everything hurts you!" Her city cracks like an earthen bowl, or Cyrano's poor head, or Pandora's box, and all the darkness in the world pours out. Then the poet invokes her muse: "May nothing, my dear, hurt you... But the thunder."

And so, as her field of reference widens, as she wearily entertains invasion by the world, its news cameras, and its indifference (I should say, in our defense, that we sent a few brave writers there, too), her own early poems turn on her. "It's not something you die of," she wrote in "Paper Tea," "waiting for evening to fall..." But of course that is exactly what her neighbors *were* dying of, huddled in their dark hallways and cellars.

Durakovic invokes those thunderous post-modernists, Hemingway and Lee Marvin, and snubs her nose at their prolix genres by entombing them in haiku. She immortalizes a visiting French lecturer to the city in a poem whose irony and fresh blood is soaked in a darkness that all of us must hope we never have to see. But *she* sees it, she writes, "in graves already covered in tireless grass," the "weeds" Lorca wrote of in "Omega," his poem for the dead Early in the book, she roams through Lorca's landscape in a poem, "Federico's Song," that is lit by "the lightning that cuts our sky into night and night." In cold, chiseled premonition, soldiers march through that poem: Lorca's gypsy killers, Hitler's SS, the neo-Chekists of Mladic and Karadzic. Then the poet's sad world-weariness sets in with a vengeance. "We know the roads. They're all the same./ Death stayed behind us, which means/ that it awaits us before we arrive,/ each at his own Cordoba."

When *Heart of Darkness* begins, the poet is hoping to be an inconspicuous speck at the crossroads of life and death, while fountains are busily modulating the thunder. (She wants to be inconspicuous, but not ineffectual or disengaged. Her definition of madness is "forgetting the dark depths/ of the carriers of the day.") At the book's end, she's sitting above a beach in Oregon, imagining that in the power of the thundering surf, before which she is once again a mere dot, she might find the strength to rewrite the history of the seige of Sarajevo the way an absent-minded J.R.R. Tolkein might rewrite the ending of one of his fabulous tales. "I think I deserve it," she writes. "I have been a good girl."

—Greg Simon
Portland, Oregon
December 1997

AUTHOR'S NOTES,
ACKNOWLEDGMENTS & COMMENTARY

A Tiny Morning with a Dedication to S.: Perun is an ancient pagan divinity, the Slavic god of thunder.

A Writer Perceives His Homeland: Tabut is a wooden board on which, according to Islamic customs, the body of the deceased is placed, covered with white sheets, and buried.

Ten Year Old Girl Perceives Her Homeland: This poem was "thought up" and written in English during my stay at The Sitka Center for Art and Ecology, in Otis, Oregon. I did not feel at home there until the day I boarded the private plane of a man who turned out to be an undertaker. He told me that only when we were high up in the sky. Which means that all places are equal, only Sarajevo is more equal to death. So I got back to my hometown,. Sarajevo, forever.

Most of these poems were published in the book *Srce tame* (Heart of Darkness) Bosanska knjiga in Sarajevo, 1993. A few of them were changed in the process of translating them into English, and new poems were added in 1996 and 1997.

The title is, of course, borrowed. I thank Joseph Conrad, who realized long before others that darkness had a heart, and that the heart had darkness, although in the end everything comes to THE HORROR! THE HORROR! THE HORROR!

This selection was made from four books of poetry, one of them unpublished, and the result is a desire to establish and perhaps to learn the difference between the twenty-year-old student of literature and the thirty-six-year-old candidate for burial on the soccer field. The difference in the heart is not big, but is essential in the darkness of the heart: this darkness is far less thick than the young one. Simply because expectations have become boundlessly small, so that life dreams have come down to water, health, home, books, and peace instead of Endeavor, History, Fame, and Love, and with capital letters besides.

I would like to thank:

Phil A. Robinson and Chris Merrill, who have made my kind of American dream come true.

Amela Simic and Zoran Mutic, who translated my Bosnian insomnia into my kind of American dream.

Bea and Del, Randall and Kim, Frank, and all the people gathered around The Sitka Center for Art and Ecology in Otis, Oregon, who made me think that, in spite of Bosnian reality, there is something good in human nature.

My Mother, Farah, and Mirza, who made me believe in me.

–F.D.

THE TERRA INCOGNITA SERIES:
WRITING FROM CENTRAL EUROPE

Series Editor: Aleš Debeljak

Volume 4
Afterwards: Slovenian Writing 1945-195
Edited by Andrew Zawacki
250 pages $17.00

Volume 3
Heart of Darkness
Poems by Ferida Durakovic
112 pages $14.00

Volume 2
The Road to Albasan
An Essay by Edmund Keeley
116 pages $14.00

Volume 1
The Four Questions of Melancholy
New and Selected Poems of Tomaž Šalamun
Edited by Christopher Merrill
266 pages $15.00

ABOUT WHITE PINE PRESS

Established in 1973, White Pine Press is a non-profit publishing house dedicated to enriching our literary heritage; promoting cultural awareness, understanding, and respect; and, through literature, addressing social and human rights issues. This mission is accomplished by discovering, producing, and marketing to a diverse circle of readers exceptional works of poetry, fiction, non-fiction, and literature in translation from around the world. Through White Pine Press, authors' voices reach out across cultural, ethnic, and gender boundaries to educate and to entertain.

To insure that these voices are heard as widely as possible, White Pine Press arranges author reading tours and speaking engagements at various colleges, universities, organizations, and bookstores throughout the country. White Pine Press works with colleges and public schools to enrich curricula and promotes discussion in the media. Through these efforts, literature extends beyond the books to make a difference in a rapidly changing world.

As a non-profit organization, White Pine Press depends on support from individuals, foundations, and government agencies to bring you important work that would not be published by profit-driven publishing houses. Our grateful thanks to the many individuals who support this effort as Friends of White Pine Press and to the following organizations: Amter Foundation, Ford Foundation, Korean Culture and Arts Foundation, Lannan Foundation, Lila Wallace-Reader's Digest Fund, Margaret L. Wendt Foundation, Mellon Foundation, National Endowment for the Arts, New York State Council on the Arts, Trubar Foundation, Witter Bynner Foundation, the Slovenian Ministry of Culture, The U.S.-Mexico Fund for Culture, and Wellesley College.

Please support White Pine Press' efforts to present voices that promote cultural awareness and increase understanding and respect among diverse populations of the world. Tax-deductible donations can be made to:

White Pine Press
P.O. Box 236, Buffalo, New York 14201